Inspiring Women

Every Day

January

WALK THIS WAY

JEN BAKER

February

HE'S IN THE WAITING

CLAIRE MUSTERS

Jen Baker

Jen Baker is a speaker, author and leader who loves seeing the Holy Spirit and the Word change lives. Called from America to live in England, Jen has been a pastor, director and consultant working with the local church and several anti-trafficking charities.

Claire Musters

Claire Musters is a writer, speaker and editor. Her recent books include *Grace-Filled Marriage* and *Every Day Insights: Disappointment and Loss.* She writes and edits regularly for magazines including *Woman Alive* and *Premier Christianity*, and writes for Bible study notes such as *Day by Day with God* and *Inspiring Women Every Day*. She also blogs at clairemusters.com

 Published by Waverley Abbey Resources. Waverley Abbey Resources is an operating name of CWR, Waverley Abbey House, Waverley Lane, Farnham, Surrey GU9 8EP, UK. Tel: 01252 784700 Email: mail@waverleyabbey.org
Registered Charity No. 294387. Registered Limited Company No. 1990308.
Front cover image: Adobe Stock Images
Concept development, editing, design and production by Waverley Abbey Resources. Printed in England by Yeomans.

Weekend

Walk this Way

JEN BAKER

Matthew 14:22–33

'"Lord, if it's you," Peter replied, "tell me to come to you on the water." "Come," he said.' (vv28–29)

Familiar stories can easily become old news. Have you ever skipped ahead in your Bible reading thinking to yourself, 'I already know what this says'? We all have! Yet God is a master at reframing the familiar into the fresh. As the dawn of a new year arises we turn our focus towards the power of taking one step, walking in the way of those who have travelled before us. We will study four ordinary people trusting an extraordinary God. As they risked stepping into unknown territory, so can we as we step into 2022.

Our weekend readings will focus on stepping *up*, *out*, *towards* and *into*. This month begins with a well known Bible story where we see Peter's boldness in choosing to step out when wisdom cautions to stay in. Globally we have had a perilous few years which, for many people, have necessitated a pulling back and, potentially, a deepened sense of caution. With that in mind, what would it look like for you to follow the Lord's command to *come* this year? Perhaps it's time to shift from personal insecurity to providential invitation. It begins with just one step.

Optional further reading

John Ortberg, *If You Want to Walk on Water, You've Got to Get Out of the Boat* (Grand Rapids, MI: Zondervan, 2001)

Bartimaeus

Mark 10:46–52

'He began to shout, "Jesus, Son of David, have mercy on me!"' (v47)

What causes you to shout? At the time of writing, England has recently lost the final of the Euro2020. A week prior to this I knew so little about football that I thought we were playing in the World Cup. Despite my woeful lack of football knowledge, on the eve of 11 July I found myself in a frenzied state, heart racing, eyes bulging, shouting at the television. This was not life and death nor did it affect my personal life in the slightest, and yet my emotions were wound tighter than a teenager on their first date. Quite simply, within a week I was swept up in the agony of a country waiting since 1966 to see their men win a major football championship.

The longer we wait, often the stronger the emotion. Trying for a child is exciting... until it has been three years and you are still trying. Waiting for a husband causes your heart to flutter... until you pass childbearing age and that same heart now sits broken and bruised. Longing for a loved one to be saved starts with faith-filled prayers... until years go by and you wonder if God is listening. Blind Bartimaeus had been waiting years to see what he could only imagine. Even with the passing of time notes of hope stirred in his heart, one day erupting into shouts reverberating louder than the lack of faith around him. The sound drew the Messiah's attention. Again, *what causes you to shout?* As we study this man who stepped away from limitation, defied the odds and received a miracle, consider what barriers might keep you from stepping into this year with faith. Will you shout today for a victory you might see tomorrow?

For prayer and reflection

Lord, thank You for hearing our cries. Whether shouts of joy or sorrow, You hear them all. Give me courage to speak the hidden desires of my heart once again. Amen.

Are you **all in**?

Luke 9:1–6

'Take nothing for the journey – no staff, no bag, no bread, no money, no extra shirt.' (v3)

I vividly remember our family holidays, riding in the back seat arguing with my sister because she had crossed the line into 'my side' of the seat. Mum had asked us to bring a few toys for the duration of our trip, so my 'friends' and I needed room. I battled tremendous insecurity as a child and had over one hundred (yes, really!) stuffed animals in my bedroom... many on my bed with me. They brought me comfort and my little heart loved them dearly. Therefore, I agonised over which animals would come with me and who I must leave behind.

This was always a struggle for my sensitive heart, but not so for Blind Bartimaeus. He chose to throw off the comfort of his coat the minute Jesus gave an invitation to come forward. I've heard it taught that this coat was a beggar's coat and, if true, then he threw it off with a faith that declared this was the last minute of his previous season. What boldness! Whether it symbolised poverty or simply provided warmth, Bartimaeus decided that where he was headed was not in line with an old garment.

We read in Hebrews 12:1, 'Therefore, since we are surrounded by such a great cloud of witnesses, let us throw off everything that hinders and the sin that so easily entangles. And let us run with perseverance the race marked out for us.' Stepping into a new season offers the opportunity to discard old habits, mindsets, grievances and prejudices. This year, will you choose to walk at a higher level of integrity, justice, conviction and grace? It might require you to cross a line of comfort but could lead you on a road to freedom.

For prayer and reflection

Lord, I know there may be areas of my life that give me comfort in place of the Comforter. Please show me what I need to release and give me the grace to let go. Amen.

Are you **honourable**?

Romans 12:10–21

'Be devoted to one another in love. Honour one another above yourselves.' (v10)

Though he had no sight, Bartimaeus carried great vision. This vision vividly comes to life when we read how he cried out, 'Son of David, have mercy on me', intentionally declaring and honouring Jesus as the Messiah. How can a blind man see what those with sight were blinded to? Yes, he had heard the stories, but hearing was not what set him free – it was *faith* that removed the stone of blindness, ushering in the light of freedom. (Mark 10:52). Bartimaeus honoured the authority that Jesus walked in because, as he heard the stories, his spirit was awakened to the freedom Jesus carried. And once awake, he refused to spend one more day asleep.

Honour opens doors and replaces limitation with possibility. It allows us to see what fear, judgment, insecurity or offence may have veiled. Where there has been a wall between us and another person, honour creates a door… or at least the possibility of one. I heard Danny Silk, author, speaker and leader at Bethel Church, once say, 'We don't honour because they are honourable but because we are'. In other words, our honour is not based on another person's integrity but on our own. We see honour written in the Ten Commandments as the first commandment that carries a promise attached to its action when we honour our parents (Exod. 20:12) Is there anyone in your life that you have failed to honour? Might this be the year to make amends? Imagine the Bride of Christ seeing with the eyes of Bartimaeus, visualising what does not yet exist. Only when we do this will there be scope for unity in place of conformity and love in place of judgment.

For prayer and reflection

Ask the Holy Spirit if there is anyone in your life you need to honour. Repent and seek forgiveness if necessary, then express honour through word or action.

Journeying to Easter:

Every Day with Jesus

Lent at Waverley Abbey Trust

- Lent retreats following the last week of Jesus' life
- Devotional material
- Books and online resources

To find out more visit

waverleyabbeyresources.org/lent-2022

THURS **JAN 6**

The power of **persistence**

Luke 18:1–8

'Jesus told his disciples a parable to show them that they should always pray and not give up.' (v1)

Observe any three-year-old and you will discover that the only limitation to persistence is found in the patience of the receiver! Until patience is exhausted, persistence will do what it does best... unremitting repetition (such as, 'Are we there yet?' for hours on end while travelling for a family holiday). Despite its dubious reputation, stubbornness is often a worthy character trait which may get chipped away through disappointment as we mature. One unanswered prayer request here, a rejection there, and a dream unfulfilled over there slowly eradicates our sense of expectation and belief. After too many seasons of hurt and disappointment we can find ourselves praying halfheartedly, hoping vainly and seeking sparingly.

In Bartimaeus, however, we find one who refused to limit himself in the midst of his limitation. Ignoring the reprimands of those around him to be silent, he cried out all the louder. There are times persistence needs to be promoted from praying to proclaiming – and then from proclaiming to responding. As we saw yesterday, the moment Jesus gave him attention excitement took over and his feet took off. He could not have known that this was the day persistence would present him with the key to his freedom, but he was ready.

Keep praying. Stay hopeful. Never give up. Stand on the Scriptures. Believe what the still small voice has spoken to you in the dark of the night. Persevere as we see not only in Bartimaeus but also in the widow from today's reading. In other words, have the faith and persistence of a three-year-old on their way to grandma's house.

For prayer and reflection

Lord, show me where disappointments are hindering my prayers of faith. I choose to cast off limitations of unbelief and, like the widow, I will believe. Amen.

What do you **want**?

FRI **JAN 7**

In John 5 we read the well known story about the man at the Pool of Bethesda who had been lying there for 38 years. Jesus meets him and promptly asks, 'Do you want to get well?' (v6). It seems a ridiculous question for someone who had been stuck for most of his life in a place he didn't want to be in, living a life unfulfilled and less than his deepest potential. Yet how many of us find ourselves in that place with the Lord? He approaches our somewhat stationary lives, asking us, *What do you want?* Do you want to believe for a new tomorrow after the devastation of yesterday? Do you want to expect blessing and prosperity in place of toil and frustration? Do you want to step towards your dream and stop circling that mountain of rejection?

Contrast this encounter with this week's study when Jesus asked Bartimaeus what he wanted. With the blind man, there was no hesitation or confusion. He knew *exactly* what he wanted because he had been imagining it all his life: he wanted to see! He wanted to behold what the years had held back. Colours, family members, a sunset and his own reflection were all waiting to step out of his imagination into his reality. Blind Bartimaeus wanted all that life had to give him and none of what the enemy had stolen from him. Ironically, a blind man could see what a sighted man could not. As we dip our toe into the edge of a new year, consider which man resembles most where you have been and where you are going. As a consequence, would you say that you are asking, seeking or knocking in this season of life?

Mark 11:22–24; Matthew 7:7–12

'Ask and it will be given to you; seek and you will find; knock and the door will be opened' (v7)

For prayer and reflection

Lord, as I imagine You asking me what I want, please help me see what my circumstances may have clouded over the years. I pray for clarity and wisdom. Amen.

Step up

John 5:1–15

'Then Jesus said to him, 'Get up! Pick up your mat and walk.' (v8)

Last weekend we saw Peter step out of the boat, and today we are reminded of what we studied yesterday when Jesus challenged a lame man to step *up* into his new season. Remember, this was not any man but a man who had likely been in a position he didn't choose, for a length of time he didn't want, living a life that wasn't free. I wonder if he had remained hopeful for the first ten years? Fifteen? Every time the waters stirred he must have had a moment of expectation, only to have that belief dashed against the rocks of shame and sorrow at not being the first into the pool. Perhaps he wondered why he wasn't chosen? What sin had he or his family committed to put him in this position? When he opened his eyes that prosaic, yet providential, morning he couldn't have known grace was about to arrive in front of his mat. Even so… he still had to rise. He had to pick up that which represented his old season. By doing this, he discovered that the waters of familiarity didn't hold his answer or his future – Jesus did.

Optional further reading

Take some time to read Joshua 1:1–9 and Joshua 3:1–5 while considering what Joshua had to pick up, leave behind and step towards. What can you learn from this?

Nicodemus

John 3:1–4

'"How can this be?" Nicodemus asked.' (v9)

It was a typical Saturday evening around 10pm when I walked into the kitchen and the ordinary quickly turned extraordinary. At arm's reach above my head was a swirling cloud that filled the whole length of the kitchen. It was so thick I couldn't see through it. I quickly surmised this wasn't smoke nor was it coming from the ceiling or walls – it was the unexplainable invading the conventional. I knew that there have been many sightings of a 'cloud of glory' over past (and current) generations... but in my *kitchen*, Lord?

We are made in God's image (Gen. 1:26) and are called to live by faith (Rom. 1:17), declaring what is not seen to be seen (Heb. 11:1; Rom. 4:17). Yet let's be honest – our natural minds still seek an explanation for what cannot be understood. Nicodemus, a Pharisee, finds himself in that position one dark evening, discussing eternity with the eternal one, seeking to comprehend what his peers could only condemn. The courage it took Nicodemus to step into that conversation cannot be underestimated. Faith often requires bravery to see beyond the popular into the possible. We must become comfortable with the fact that we will be misunderstood as followers of Christ; a truth that I believe gathers strength with every passing year and generation. I have tried to explain away that cloud, but have concluded there is no explanation. So I surrender to the prospect that God can do what He wants, when He wants, in the manner that He wants. Quite simply, I want my seeking to land me in the arena of 'trust and obey' even if I'm shrouded in a cloud of 'I don't understand'.

For prayer and reflection

Lord, some things I do not understand about Your ways and my circumstances. I ask for grace to help me trust Your great love, shown in John 3:16 so poignantly. Amen.

TUES **JAN 11**

Genesis 17:1–8; 2 Corinthians 9:8–11

'You will have more than enough of everything—every moment and in every way.' (2 Cor. 9:8, TPT)

More than enough

There are various interpretations of God's name, El-Shaddai (first spoken in Genesis 17:1). A few of the most common are that He is the 'God Almighty' while others interpret the name to mean 'All Sufficient One'. We also know Him as creator, and by putting these together we see a God who can create with might and sufficiency. In other words, even darkness cannot stand against His capacity to produce something more than is seen in the moment, as we read in Genesis 1.

This ability to produce beyond what is currently understood can be found through the subtext of Nicodemus' conversation with Jesus. In other words, what is currently known is not all there is to know. This awareness releases questions for each of us. Are we seeking more? Have we become complacent in our knowledge of the Holy One? Are we sitting on the throne of doctrine over the thrill of unity?

Stepping towards more understanding is vital to the life of a believer who wants to stay hungry and thirsty for righteousness. In the natural our hunger prompts us to ask for more, but do we reflect this in our spiritual lives? Am I asking for more of His presence, more intimacy in prayer, more wisdom from the Word and more unity with those from denominations other than my own? We serve a God of *more than enough* yet we are often satisfied with just enough. If darkness couldn't stand against this name, why should poverty, sickness, prejudice, evil or jealousy? Seeking answers to these and other questions often unveils insights we may not have known we carried. Like Nicodemus, may we never lose our wonder of a wonder-full God.

For prayer and reflection

Consider what 'more' means to you. Do you desire more wisdom, discernment, intimacy, direction? Pray believing that He is sufficient to supply and eager to bless.

Mind the **gap**

John 3:4–17; Ephesians 2:4–10

'God is spirit, and his worshippers must worship in the Spirit and in truth.' (John 4:24)

Recently I saw a BBC report of a man in India who saved a young boy that had accidentally fallen onto train tracks in front of an oncoming train. His mother, who was blind, was screaming in terror as she could not see him to save him, yet thirteen seconds of nail-biting video footage shows a man willing to give up his life to save the life of another. The video reveals a gap too wide for little legs to stretch and a darkness too great for his mother to cross.

Nicodemus senses a similar gap when he questions how a person can re-enter his mother's womb – an impossibility in anyone's belief system! At the beginning of their dialogue, Nicodemus nails his colours to the mast by declaring only God could do the miracles Jesus had been doing; yet Jesus knows that this revelation is still not enough to bridge the gap residing in his heart. As the mother could not save what she could not see, our strength and desire is not enough to close the gap between us and heaven. There is another who ran towards us, before our fall, sacrificing His life for our freedom.

As they talked, Nicodemus equally learned that it was impossible to close this gap through religion or good works. As we envision a year of possibility, are we seeing through the eyes of achievement or grace? Are we already striving for the approval we hope to receive in December for a year well lived, or are we resting in the truth that God's love is not based on outward success? Nicodemus learned that there are some gaps only grace can cross, reminding me of the hymn that beautifully declares we once were blind, but now we see.

For prayer and reflection

Take a few moments to remember (or sing) the words found in the familiar hymn *Amazing Grace.* Choose one verse to meditate on, thanking Jesus for bridging that gap.

Learn to be the Difference

You'll find space to learn and grow alongside a strong Christian heritage.

Waverley Abbey College provides training that ranges from one day seminars up to five-year part-time Higher Education courses, within three faculties:

- Counselling
- Spiritual Formation
- Leadership

To find out more about our courses, come and visit us on an open day. Register your interest now: **waverleyabbeycollege.ac.uk/open-days/**

Take a look at a selection of our offering...

Learn to be the Difference

Introduction to Christian Care and Counselling

This five-day course introduces you to the practical methods and theory in counselling and pastoral care.

Coaching and Mentoring

Develop your skills as coach or mentor with the Postgraduate Certificate in Mentoring and Coaching.

Chaplaincy

In whichever context you'd like to serve, our distance learning course in Contemporary Chaplaincy will equip you with the skills you need.

Leadership

New! This faculty launched in January, with two distance learning courses:

- MA in Public Leadership; and
- Certificate and Diploma of Higher Education in Integrating Faith and Leadership

THURS **JAN 13**

Confronting the **darkness**

Matthew 26:36–46; Ephesians 6:10–18

'Finally, be strong in the Lord and in his mighty power.' (v10)

Vast darkness has never threatened the vitality of God's light. As we saw on Tuesday, within the first few lines of creation's opening act darkness bows to the authority of heaven (Gen 1:1–3), the latter shattering any illusion that a long night holds precedence over a new day. That being said, there are lessons to be learnt in seasons of shadow that mountaintops cannot mirror. Nicodemus came to Jesus at night likely, though not definitively, because he did not want his colleagues seeing him conversing with the greatest perceived threat to their well rehearsed religion As a darkroom brings out the hues of a photograph, darkness provided enough cover for answers to begin emerging on the heart of one man's curiosity.

I would never want to repeat the dark nights of the soul which seemed to appear out of nowhere, sideswiping me out of life's rhythm and into a screeching halt of confusion, uncertainty and doubt. Yet, on the other side of those same seasons I have seen through a new lens, carrying a fresh anointing that familiarity could not bring. If you find yourself in a dark season now, or this year, may I gently encourage you to allow that time to reveal what perhaps would not otherwise be seen in the light of comfort and ease. Where you find yourself confused around God's ways, seek His nature. you are wrestling with grief over life's cruelty, seek His comfort. When there is pain or rejection from one you love, seek His companionship. The more we seek Him in our darkness, the greater He will appear in His light, painting a picture only heaven could create.

For prayer and reflection

Lord, no darkness is too dark for You. Thank You for meeting me in my dark places, sitting with me there, and showing me the way out when I am ready. Amen.

Standing **alone**

FRI **JAN 14**

Matthew 10:26–33; 16:24–26

'So do not be afraid of them.' (v26)

In a world that is rife with confused identities, perceptions, prejudices and ideologies, the need for courageous kingdom voices has never been greater. Having wisdom about when to speak and when to be silent is growing more necessary with every passing year. Silence in some settings appears louder than a jet plane; yet vehemently voicing judgment may silently expose the depth of one's pride. Therefore, gaining clarity on a situation may first require us to step out of the crowd and away from the lure of both silence and judgment.

Wisdom seeks truth before voicing opinion – and Nicodemus was a wise man. He took time to seek out truth, albeit at night, before he made a decision on this Jesus who he was hearing did miracles. Have you allowed judgment to obscure seeking? Or silence to camouflage speaking? There are some truths that don't need to be confirmed – such as the truth of loving our neighbour regardless of race; standing up for righteousness whatever the cost; and caring for poor, hungry and destitute people despite their choices.

After this nighttime rendezvous we later see Nicodemus attempting to assist Jesus, at the personal cost of the jeers from his peers (John 7:51–52). The final curtain is drawn on Nicodemus' role in Christ's story when we see him joining Joseph of Arimathea to bury Jesus' body in a rich man's tomb, embalmed with a generous mixture of myrrh and aloes (John 19:38-40). An extravagant offering fit for the King of all kings, provided by a man who, in the end, chose to seek and to serve where others were content to hunt and to kill.

For prayer and reflection

Lord, please reveal to me areas of my heart that harbour judgment and prejudice. Forgive me for holding grievances and give me eyes to see others as You see them. Amen.

Weekend

Step out of slavery

John 11:1–6, 32–44

'Jesus called in a loud voice, "Lazarus, come out!"' (v43)

This can be your year. Your year to make that choice, take that job, instigate that phone call, forgive that person, write that book, raise that child, pay off that debt, love that neighbour, join that team or mend that relationship. Regardless of how long we have been held back by a lie, trauma, sin or shame there is nothing stronger than the freedom given to us through Jesus Christ at the cross. Yes, there are some things that might take a lifetime to process and navigate, but our current position does not define our future posture. Freedom often comes in stages and steps. Lazarus was free, but he was still bound and needed others to step in and untangle what was holding him back.

You might be Lazarus, needing courage to stand up and take that first step *out* of darkness towards the voice of freedom. Alternatively, you might be the onlooker hearing Jesus invite you to step forward out of comfort, releasing one who is unable to free themselves from their current cobweb of wrong choices or unjust circumstances.

Where are you standing and which step will you take?

Optional further reading

Romans 8; 1 Corinthians 13:4–6

The Shunnamite

2 Kings 4:8–17

'No, my lord!' she objected. 'Please, man of God, don't mislead your servant!' (v15)

Have you ever had something spoken that was 'too good to be true'? Perhaps it was the man you loved asking for your hand in marriage, the adoption agency calling with the news that a child is matched or the doctor giving you the all clear. For some, you have dared to hope for so many years that to receive what you have longed for seems hard to believe at best and a cruel joke at worst. That posture of inconceivable is where the Shunnamite finds herself when talking to the prophet Elisha. Her dream of bearing a child seemed to have died long ago; therefore she was now 'sufficient' (v13, AMPC) in her surroundings. Yet, we were never created to dwell in sufficiency.

Handling disappointment is too big a topic for a devotional of this length. Instead, we will explore the metamorphosis of language as she steps away from what she had always known into what she had once dreamed. As we go along, consider your own story. Are there any areas where you have settled for sufficiency, when deep down you desire the exceeding and above that you once imagined (Eph. 3:20)?

Being 52-years old, never married, and with no children has necessitated me navigating years of disappointment, doubt, unanswered questions and halfhearted hope. I know what it feels like to do all the 'right' things and yet still feel heaven has rejected you for reasons beyond your understanding. Equally, I know the power of choice and the potential of voice to shift atmospheres and create opportunities. Before we continue, take a moment to consider if you are *sitting in sufficiency* or *walking in fidelity* when it comes to faith.

For prayer and reflection

Lord, as I give You my fears, concerns and disappointments, I believe You hold them close. Where I lack trust, please help me to rest in Your love and grace. Amen.

TUES **JAN 18**

Where are you **going**?

2 Kings 4:18–22; Mark 5:35–42

'She went up and laid him on the bed of the man of God, then shut the door and went out.' (v21)

I like to call this woman our 'Dynamite Shunammite' because I sense that she was a woman of strength, courage, leadership and tenacity. I can't prove it but I tend to think she was a force to be reckoned with, in the nicest possible way, and that her husband loved that about her! Therefore, when the dream she had been waiting for all her life suddenly died, she did not go into self-pity but she sought spiritual help. Interestingly, she did not tell her husband what had happened, instead choosing to take control of the situation and arrange to speak with Elisha – the one responsible for awakening a hope inside her that had long been sleeping. Who do you run to when disaster strikes? What words come out of your mouth when fear knocks at your door? How do you see the Lord when faced with a sudden dead-end?

In crisis, we will always show outwardly what has been growing inwardly. You may find that in seasons of prosperity and joy God seems to grow more silent, making it easier to drift and enjoy the lack of battle instead of strengthening your fight muscles, preparing you for what's ahead. I am not trying to appear negative by saying this, but as believers we will *always* have battles to fight if we are living from another kingdom. This dynamite woman might have rejected pity due to her headstrong personality, but she still had to choose. She ran *towards* the one who could help her and, as we will see this week, she demanded what he had promised. If you have a dream that has died, I would encourage you to lay it on the bed of hope, choosing to approach the promise-giver for direction.

For prayer and reflection

Are you allowing your spiritual tank to be filled with faith, ready for future challenges? Meditate on this picture and hear what the Spirit says to you in this season.

All is **well**

WED **JAN 19**

2 Kings 4:23–26; Psalm 46

'She said, "All is well."' (v23, ESVUK)

I think one of the most challenging aspects of faith is to silence fear with our trust. We can struggle to fully put ourselves out there, leaning wholly on the Lord while we stand on the water of faith without a life vest of works to bail us out if it all goes wrong. Where is the line between not having a 'plan B' yet also not abdicating our responsibility to use the gifts with which God has entrusted us? In this week's Bible story, we see a woman walking that tightrope beautifully. Clearly there was fear in her heart when the son she had believed for took his last breath, but there was faith in her voice when she answered the questions with *all is well.*

Long before I knew this phrase was famously penned by Julian of Norwich, I wrote it in large letters on a whiteboard in my office. At that time I was leading a team facing numerous challenges and, as the leader, I was personally facing obstacles I had never faced before, unsure how to lead and stretched beyond my capacity. Over the years this phrase has stayed with me, and I regularly repeat it to myself and others. Words are powerful, bringing either life or death to our atmospheres and circumstances (Proverbs 18:21). We would be wise to watch how we speak when we aren't under pressure, using spiritual disciplines to strengthen our faith for seasons when pressure races towards us like a car without breaks. As we memorise scriptures, read the Word, pray in natural words or a spiritual language, fast, and have Sabbath days of rest, we are declaring with each discipline, 'Yes, all truly *is* well'.

For prayer and reflection

Lord, I long to trust You at a deeper level, knowing that resting in You is the safest place I can reside. I receive Your peace now as I wait in Your presence. Amen.

THURS **JAN 20**

Stubborn faith

2 Kings 4:27–37

'As surely as the LORD lives and as you live, I will not leave you.' (v30)

When our heart breaks, our dream dies and our future appears to cease we can be tempted to push stop instead of pause. First, let me emphasise that there are seasons to grieve, and that some trauma rests within our soul until we see our Saviour face to face – and that is OK. I am not insinuating that you rush what God is restoring. But when the time is right and the Spirit nudges, wisdom walks with determination towards the only one who can truly answer our heart cry – Jesus.

During one intensely painful season of my life I heard the Lord say three words: 'I've got you'. That helped me hold on by my fingertips when I felt like I was hovering over a chasm too deep to survive if I lost my grip and fell. *Repeatedly* I asked Him if He was still there with me? Without fail I would hear Him say, 'I've got you'. Why wasn't once enough? Because in sorrow we need reassurance. We need to know that this season will not last forever and, though it seems impossible, a sunrise *will* follow what may be the longest storm of our life. When time stands still and grief swallows faith, ask Him for a word.

Our Dynamite Shunnamite chose to stay with the man who held the healing her crisis required. Once she stepped towards him she would not walk away without him. In her declaration (v30) she gives us a blueprint of faith for seasons of fear. Stand with Him when all else has failed; stand with Him when all others are silent; stand with Him when all around you is chaos; stand with Him when all you know has changed. Perhaps this is your 2022 declaration: 'As surely as You live, Lord, I will not leave You'.

For prayer and reflection

Lord, I choose to declare my trust in You at the start of this year. As Proverbs 3:5–6 says, I will trust You with all my heart. Thank You for directing my paths. Amen.

The **final** word

2 Kings 8:1–6

'At the end of the seven years she came back' (v3)

Our back story is never our full story, it is only part of the story. Regardless of your background, upbringing, start to life or choices along the way, if you are reading this your story is not yet finished. One thing I have learned after 30 years of walking with the Lord is that those seasons which held our darkest moments often become seeds producing our greatest victories. It reminds me of a well known verse found in Genesis 50:20, where Joseph who was sold into slavery by his brothers declares, 'You intended to harm me, but God intended it for good to accomplish what is now being done, the saving of many lives.' God always has the final word.

As seen in the Bible reading for today, the Shunammite's family (her son having been raised back to life by Elisha) had to leave their home owing to a famine, returning seven years later. Imagine seven years' wondering what was happening to your home and your land. Would it be taken over by someone else? Would looters come in and steal your belongings while you were away? Would the ground still be fertile enough to produce a harvest? Space won't permit more than to say than that *God's timing is stunning.* The moment she and her son approach the king to learn of their future, Elisha's servant 'happens' to be explaining to the king about her son's resurrection from the dead. The king was so impressed she immediately received all that she had lost, including income from the time she was away. Amazing!

What is due you that has been stolen over the years? Perhaps this is the year to approach the King, believing for recompense and open to abundance.

For prayer and reflection

Think about what has been stolen from you over the years and ask the Holy Spirit to show you what He desires to give you in return. Then pray a bold prayer in faith!

Towards the King

Esther 4:9–5:3; Matthew 16:13–20

'So Esther approached and touched the tip of the sceptre.' (v2)

I wonder how often we stop to consider the undeniable, inconceivable privilege we have as believers that we can approach the King of kings at any moment, day or night. We don't need to wait for a summons or write a note requesting an audience… we only need to approach. Esther put her life in danger to do in front of a man what we, without fear, do in front of a holy and all-powerful God. Aside from the obvious, what is the greatest difference between the two? Love.

Love beckons us forward, not power. Love seeks our company, not lust. Love keeps the door open, not will. It is God's love that draws us, and ultimately His love that will keep us in the kingdom for all of eternity.

We cannot escape the love of the Father in the same way trees cannot escape the touch of the wind. Being planted in His kingdom commits us to a life of love which overwhelms us without ceasing, for all eternity, demonstrated through the Father, Son and Holy Spirit. As we meditate on this truth over the weekend, allow its invitation to draw you *towards* the King. And as you draw closer, consider what your request will be?

Optional further reading

Jen Baker, *Face to Face* (Milton Keynes, Bucks: Authentic Media, 2019)

Short Courses

One day courses. No entry requirements. £59.50 each

Courses include...

7 Imperatives in Troubled Times

How to lead in turbulent circumstances.

Bible in a Day

Navigate the Bible. Learn tools for wise interpretation and application. Read the Bible for all it's worth.

Quest for a way of life that works

Find a way to root your spirituality in your day-to-day life

Renewing your Mind: What the Bible says

How has God has equipped us all to become like Christ? Discover how the Bible's view of the mind overlaps with the latest teaching of neuro science.

For more courses, information and to sign up today visit our website **waverleyabbeyresources/courses**

MON **JAN 24**

The widow

Mark 12:41–44; Ephesians 2:6–7

'A poor widow came and put in two very small copper coins, worth only a few pence.' (v42)

So far, we have stepped away from limitation, confusion and disappointment. We will finish by studying a somewhat minor (yet powerful) woman who teaches us about stepping away from insignificance. This was a woman who had experienced loss, grief, heartache, poverty and, I imagine, loneliness. She was a widow in an age and culture that made her dependent on others for her survival. *She was also noticed by heaven.*

Our measure of worth in the world and in the kingdom are as different as the Scottish Highlands are to the London streets. What our culture deems significant pales in comparison to what catches Jesus' attention. Measuring my worth through the lens of culture will obscure heaven's applause, potentially weakening earth's impact. While we know these truths, living them in a world bent on comparison becomes increasingly challenging. At the weekend, we read about the keys of the kingdom (Matt. 16:19) – they are yours because you are His. Your significance lies in your position, not your perfection. Hence, what are you bringing to the offering this year? What constitutes your 'two mites'? Reflect on loss you've experienced in the past few years: what can you offer from that pain, confusion or heartache?

Whatever you bring, the Lord watches closely. It may be a sacrifice of praise in the midst of personal pain or a quiet word of forgiveness in response to the harsh tones of judgment. I would encourage you to sow a seed of finance, time or other earthly treasure this week, however small, reminding yourself that nothing sacrificed this year will be missed by the loving gaze of heaven.

For prayer and reflection

Lord, thank You for the opportunity to give. I desire to quickly obey in this area and I ask Your help to be extravagant in the seeds that I sow this year. Amen.

Less may be more

2 Corinthians 9:6–11; Proverbs 11:25

'Remember: A stingy planter gets a stingy crop; a lavish planter gets a lavish crop.' (v6, *The Message*)

The Cambridge Dictionary defines generosity as 'a willingness to give help or support, esp. more than is usual or expected'.* In other words, we follow in the footsteps of our creator who does above and beyond what we can ask or even imagine (Eph. 3:20) – seeking opportunities to increase and expand, that we might be a greater conduit of blessing to others. It is counter-intuitive, but if we believe our giving is based on what we currently hold then we are instantly limited by the barrier of sight. We see this illustrated beautifully in the African impala who can jump to a height of over 10 ft (3 metres) at a distance greater than 30 ft (9 metres), yet a 3 ft (1 metre) wall keeps them enclosed, in a prison of limitation, because they cannot see where their feet will land. If we see *ourselves* as the source of how far we can go with our giving, we will never venture beyond our natural skill set or carefully crafted comfort zone.

Generosity envisions beyond the expected and ventures towards the excessive. It looks like the creator being crucified by the created; the concentration-camp victim forgiving her sister's murderer; the missionary leaving all that has been familiar for a culture wholly unfamiliar; or a widow clearing out her cupboards to provide food for a prophet. While we may not find ourselves in these exact scenarios, we do have opportunity to sacrifice, forgive, trust and give at an excessive level in this next season. It begins with a willingness to respond with a resounding 'yes' before hearing the question or seeing the answer. Will you take the leap?

*dictionary.cambridge.org/dictionary/english/generosity[accessed 23/09/2021]

For prayer and reflection

Which of the following do you find most sacrificial: forgiveness, trust, giving (eg time, talent, resources)? What would improving in this area look like for you?

WED **JAN 26**

Seasons of life

1 Timothy 4:11–16; Philippians 1:3–11

'He who began a good work in you will carry it on to completion until the day of Christ Jesus.' (v6)

The enemy loves extremes: judgmental/apathetic; fear/pride; controlling/disengaged. He is a master at taking a thread of truth and weaving it into a tapestry of deceit. Therefore, he would not hesitate to use the truth of your moment to construct a false narrative for your future. One of his greatest extremes, and deepest lies, is when he seeks to ascribe the inexperience of youth or the irrelevance of old age as a reason for us to remain on the sidelines of God's great commission. When this happens we may respond with another extreme: holding back or lunging forward. For example, we might say that we are refraining from putting ourselves forward because we are waiting on the Lord (when in reality we are afraid to look foolish or we feel out of our depth). Or we say that we would love that position because we want to serve (when in reality our identity is bound up in what we do or we're afraid of being left behind).

How do we avoid these extremes? I believe it's found by remaining in Christ *and* in community. The Word of God keeps us grounded and the right community can keep us stretched. Recently I asked one of our pastors to be my 'spiritual advisor'. I wanted to give someone permission to ask any questions about any areas of my life at any time. She surprised me by saying that she would be honoured, but she wanted to hold me accountable to my *dreams*, not just my behaviour. How beautiful!

Accountability has been misused in the past and is often seen as negative, but in the right context it can help us stay beautifully balanced... regardless of our age.

For prayer and reflection

Lord, I believe You still have plans for me that are yet to be fulfilled. I choose to say *yes* this year and focus more on who You are rather than who I am not. Amen.

Coming from **behind**

Luke 21:1–4; Hebrews 12:1–2

'but she out of her poverty put in all she had to live on.' (v4)

I became a Christian at the age of 19. At that time I was at university and I found myself overseeing a group of girls a year younger than me. The majority of them were Christians so I immediately felt self-imposed pressure to look like a good Christian around them, having no real understanding of what that even meant. The result of my insecurity was a sense that I was continually a step behind spiritually, and that others would think I was faking my spirituality – which I was! Even after many years in the ministry, hundreds of hours studying and having received my ordination, I *still* battled thoughts that I was going to embarrass myself because I wasn't as knowledgeable as those around me. Interestingly, this is a lie I have heard many others express when it comes to anything spiritual: *'I need to be silent because I might get it wrong.'*

The word 'poverty' in verse 4 comes from the Greek word *hystérēma* which can be translated as 'lacking' or 'insufficient'. It's derived from *hysteréō* which can be translated 'at the end', meaning to come behind and therefore be left out, left wanting and to fall short. Are there areas you feel that you are coming from behind, have been left out or are falling short in? Perhaps you are still single or have not yet had children? Or you are the family member with financial struggles? Maybe the health battle that has dogged you for years has kept you on the sidelines? Jesus praised the widow for using what she had to do what she could. Today let's remember, there is no coming behind in the kingdom of God, only walking alongside.

For prayer and reflection

Lord, thank You for the opportunity to honour You through my giving, however small, for all that You have given to me. I receive your smile over my life today. Amen.

FRI **JAN 28**

Strengthen your faith!

Matthew 17:14–20; Hebrews 11:1

'Nothing will be impossible for you.' (v20)

Faith sees in the spirit and steps in the natural; then waits in the natural to experience what it has seen in the spiritual. If our natural eyes can see what we desire then there is no need for faith. Similarly, feelings of insignificance cause one to shrink back while faith challenges one to step out. We have seen this outworked through a poor widow and, in our text, we see the same power of faith heal a demon-possessed boy. Jesus declares 'nothing will be impossible for you' by exerting even the smallest amount of faith. Size mattered little to the widow's offering. Equally, size seems irrelevant in the context of faith. The enemy often lies by saying 'if you had more faith you could (fill in the blank)' when in reality a little bit of faith can move an immovable mountain... and we have *all* been given a measure of faith (Rom. 12:3).

It's helpful to remember that we don't gain more muscles in the natural, we strengthen those we already have. The same applies to our faith. We aren't rewarded with more faith by our actions, but we can strengthen our faith through our choices. How have your faith muscles been strengthened recently? What weight are you carrying now that you couldn't have carried a few years ago? As a result, what can you see by faith for your future as you intentionally strengthen in this area?

All of heaven is watching to see the Bride of Christ step further into her identity and move confidently in her authority, knowing that nothing – absolutely nothing – is impossible for a God *of* the impossible. With that in mind, let's see, step, carry and overcome this year!

For prayer and reflection

Lord, today I choose to believe that You can do the impossible for me. Where I am weak, be my strength and where I am unsure, be my stability. I trust You. Amen.

More from your authors

Enjoying these notes? Get 10% off these titles from your IWED authors

Every Day Insights:
Disappointment & Loss

Unwavering

Unshakeable Confidence

Unlimited

Untangled

Insight into Burnout

Insight into
Self Acceptance

C2C David

C2C Exodus

10% off until the end of February using code

IWED2021JF waverleyabbeyresources.org/iwedoffer

Weekend

JAN 29/30

Into grace

Luke 7:36–50

'Jesus said to the woman, "Your faith has saved you; go in peace."' (v50)

We have stepped up, out, towards and now *into* where God is leading us. Taking steps looks different in each season, and with each person, but the fact remains that stepping requires movement, both metaphorically and naturally. Realistically, by December 2022 you will have been required to step into new things. For some, the new might necessitate releasing something you have held onto for many years and, for others, you may need to expand your thinking to believe yourself worthy of what God is placing before you. Each requires a level of surrender.

As we break open our own offering over the next few months, we will release a scent fragrant to some and potentially off-putting to others. One of my favourite sentences is found in verse 44 where Jesus asks Simon the Pharisee if he sees this woman. Clearly, he sees her and that is why he's appalled by her actions! It proves that we can have sight with no vision. The Church is called to be His ambassadors here on earth, seeing as our Father sees, allowing ourselves to be broken vessels His love can pour through. Are you willing to be broken?

Optional further reading

Ephesians 2:1–10; Mark 14:3–9; Isaiah 43:19

The **power** of one step

Psalm 31:1–20

'My life, my every moment, my destiny—it's all in your hands.' (v15, TPT)

This is a beautiful Psalm packed with wisdom, challenge and teaching; it also addresses the power of one step. In it, we see the footprints of David as he moves away from the enemy, walking into the abundance of God's goodness. Never underestimate the power of one step. Remember the enduring words of Neil Armstrong, 'That's one small step for man, one giant leap for mankind'? We celebrate the first steps of a young child and applaud first steps after a loved one recovers from surgery.

When Jesus was dying on the cross and about to step into the depths of hell, preceding the victory of heaven, he quoted from this Psalm by saying, 'Father, into your hands I commit my spirit' (v5); equally Stephen, before stepping into eternity, prayed, 'Lord Jesus, receive my spirit' (Acts 7:59). One declaration that I make every day is that 'my steps are ordered of the Lord and my times are in Your hands' (from Psalms 37:23 and 31:15). Since intentionally declaring these words, I have felt a deeper sense of peace, a lesser sense of urgency and a greater sense of trust that all I need to do is walk in obedience step-by-step and the master-weaving of my Father's hand will orchestrate my days into the tapestry of His desire.

We have studied the lives of a blind man, a Pharisee, a Shunnamite and a widow – each with something to say about stepping out of comfort and into calling. Who did you identify with the most? Would they have declared today's verse over their lives? Will you?

My prayer is that as we follow their examples we will experience a year of abundant opportunity and untold blessing, step-by-step.

For prayer and reflection

Lord, where I am hesitant to let go and *fully* trust You I choose now to step. With eyes fixed on You, I declare that I will let go of fear and grab hold of faith. Amen.

He's in the waiting

Claire Musters

Lamentations 3:22–26

'The LORD is my portion; therefore I will wait for him' (v24)

Waiting is not something that we are used to in our frenetic twenty-first-century world. And yet, when Covid-19 hit we were forced to wait for so many things. Used to being able to walk into a supermarket, we suddenly found long queues and empty shelves when we arrived. We had to wait many months to see those outside our households in the flesh.

I'm sure, like me, you found things about that time heartbreaking and frustrating – but perhaps also an important spiritual lesson? I found my life got even busier, at a time when I was already grieving – but then a family crisis forced me to pare back what I was doing, to wait on God and cry out for Him to act on our behalf. At the same time, I was attending daily prayer Zoom calls, standing with another family waiting for their wife/sister/daughter to wake up from a coma caused by a brain haemorrhage. Month after month was painful, confusing, exhausting – but also taught us all so much about God's faithfulness, His character and our own walk of faith before Him.

In verse 25 it says, 'the LORD is good to those whose hope is in him'. Do we really believe that? Too often, a prolonged time of waiting causes us to question whether God is good. When God says 'Wait', or we hear nothing at all, we can seek to answer our own prayers, rather than reminding ourselves that God is our portion, therefore we will wait for Him to act.

As we explore the month's theme of seeing God in the waiting, we'll learn that He always has a purpose in those 'in between', often perplexing times. Let's dig into what the Bible can teach us about waiting well.

For prayer and reflection

Lord, I know that I don't always cope well in times of waiting. I am sorry for my impatience. Soften my heart to be open to what You want to teach me. Amen.

Give to make a difference

Our Bible reading notes are read by hundreds of thousands of people around the world. *Every Day with Jesus* and *Inspiring Women Every Day* are now free in the UK. We want everyone, whatever their financial means to have access to these resources that help them walk each day with our Saviour.

It makes all the difference. One reader in Malaysia said:

When I was first exposed to Every Day with Jesus about two years ago, I could sense something different, something refreshing, and I was energised. I used to struggle to translate knowledge into my daily life. EDWJ helped me to be more insightful, more positive, and to enjoy everyday life as a disciple. This helps me to be patient and positive at home, at work, and at church.

As we trust in God's provision, we know there are costs to providing this ministry. Can you give to make a difference in someone's life? Could supporting this vision be a way in which you serve?

A gift of just £2 a month from you will put daily Bible reading notes into the hands of at least one person who is hungry to know God and experience His presence every day.

Visit **waverleyabbeytrust.org/make-a-donation** to give to make a difference, or use the form at the back of these notes.

WED **FEB 2**

Faithful waiting

Genesis 6:9–14; 7:1–5,17,24

'The waters flooded the earth for a hundred and fifty days.' (v24)

The story of Noah is one that many of us will have been familiar with since childhood. Yet how often do we stop and think about the story's details? God decided to wipe out the entire human race, apart from Noah's family, and asked him to create an ark that could house two of every animal. In faith, despite the fact that he lived in the desert, we are told that Noah set to work immediately. I wonder how quickly we respond to God's clear instructions, particularly if they seem counter-intuitive and could open us up to ridicule?

The process of building such a boat would have been arduous and long, and there must have been moments in which those he knew questioned his sanity – perhaps he did too. And even when he got every person and animal on board there would have been a wait until the rains started. They were stuck on that ark for a long time – it was over a year before they were able to disembark. Just imagine how stinky and smelly it would have been amongst so many animals – and consider the huge sense of loss, when the rains did cover the earth, as friends and neighbours died.

Through that experience Noah gained much: salvation for himself and his family. He also learned that God is true to His Word. And yet it would have been painful and costly too, and necessitated stepping out in faith and clinging to God's promise. Sometimes God asks us to step out in a specific way, and even when things happen as He told us they would, the process can be more uncomfortable and messier than we thought it would be. Do we remain as steadfast in our faith as Noah did?

For prayer and reflection

Lord, I am humbled when I consider how obedient Noah was. You called him to wait in the midst of mess; help me to be faithful in the messy times of my life. Amen.

Faith on **shaky ground**

THURS **FEB 3**

Genesis 12:1–20

'Say you are my sister, so that I will be treated well for your sake' (v13)

Abram was another biblical character with a specific calling from God who we read acted quickly and with obedience. His story is full of impressive action: he rescued Lot, pleaded for Sodom and knew the fulfilment of God's promise to make him into a great nation. And yet, as we will look at over the next few days, his actions were not always as they should have been.

It was a huge ask: to leave the home that he had always known, all those he had built community with; to take his household and begin a nomadic lifestyle until God established them as a great nation. There was a great deal of waiting involved – and hardships along the way. During a time of famine, they travelled to Egypt and it is there that Abram's faith gave way to fear. In an act of desperate self-preservation, he ended up putting his own wife in an exceedingly awkward position. I often view Pharaoh's response to him as God cleaning up the mess – pointing out his folly but also sending him on his way with more than he had arrived with.

There are times when I find myself judging biblical characters as I read about their mistakes, and yet I'm also extremely grateful for the detail in their accounts which often showed how human they truly were. How many of us can say, when we are in a season of waiting, that we've never given way to fear? I think it can be a natural response, but it is what we do next that matters. The problems occur when, rather than taking our fear to God, we allow it to fuel our actions, as Abram did. If we know that a period of waiting is causing us to fear, let's be honest before God about it.

For prayer and reflection

I am aware, God, of moments when I allow myself to be overtaken by fear. Help me to bring it before You, as I know Your perfect love casts out fear. Amen.

FRI **FEB 4**

Doing things **her way**

Genesis 16:1–6

'Go, sleep with my slave; perhaps I can build a family through her.' (v2)

We know that God had promised Abram a son (see Gen. 15) and yet time kept passing and still his wife Sarai was not pregnant. Notice she blames God for this ('The LORD has kept me from having children' – v2). We don't know the reasons why she had been unable to get pregnant, but playing the blame game, particularly when God had spoken a specific promise, would not have been helpful. It probably fuelled her thinking… and the resulting suggestion. I can just imagine her talking to herself and justifying what she did next: 'Well if God had said we would have children why is He not making it happen? Just like everything else around here, I'm going to have to organise it myself…' While it was not uncommon for childless couples to get a slave to carry a child for them, this was not what God had said would happen. She was taking control and utilising a common cultural 'solution'. However, once Hagar was pregnant Sarai didn't like the resulting attitude – and played the blame game once more. She ended up behaving so badly towards Hagar that she ran away! I am really humbled when I think of my own responses to times of waiting. I know there have been moments when I have thought I know better than God, and taken matters into my own hands. Then when I haven't liked the result, I have blamed others and taken it out on those around me. Yet, even in the worst of those moments* God did not accuse me, but gently drew me to Himself and showered me with His love.

Let's learn to recognise those moments when we are beginning to edge towards acting out of our own wisdom, rather than God's.

*For more on this story, see my books Taking off the Mask and Grace-Filled Marriage (Milton Keynes, Bucks: Authentic Media).

For prayer and reflection

Perhaps you recognise the thinking that I suggested might be going on in Sarai's head. If you know you are becoming impatient, have an honest conversation with God.

Waiting with our whole beings

Psalm 130:5–8

'I wait for the LORD, my whole being waits, and in his word I put my hope.' (v5)

We do not know who wrote this psalm, although some suggest it was Hezekiah. What I love about it is the vivid description of waiting with his 'whole being'. This is fully immersive, involving every part of him. I find it a beautiful yet hugely challenging picture. Do I wait with my whole being? What does it even mean to do such a thing? Take some time to ponder those questions for yourself today.

It reminds me that the way I think, speak and act should all be reflecting the fact that I am waiting for God rather than relying on myself. It causes me to wonder whether I am posturing myself in a way to receive what God has for me, or whether I am rushing on, looking for the answers and perhaps missing what God is doing in this very moment.

I am grateful for the reminder to put my hope in His Word (v5) and His loving character too (v8). When we are in a time of waiting, we need to be confident in whom we are trusting to act on our behalf. How well we know God's Word, His promises and His character will be revealed in such times. Do you know what is being revealed in your own life today?

Optional further reading

Psalm 33:20

MON **FEB 7**

Seen by God

Genesis 16:7–16; 21:9–20

'She gave this name to the LORD who spoke to her: "You are the God who sees me"' (16:13)

I feel quite uncomfortable about Hagar's story. Used as a pawn in her mistress's game, she was mistreated and ran away – and then was later sent away!

When she had fled, God gave her back dignity by asking her a question and then listening. But what happened next must have been hard: 'Go back to your mistress and submit to her' (v9), even though there was the promise of numerous descendants.

I alluded on Friday to a time in my own life when I took matters into my own hands and then struggled deeply with the result, I still had a choice. Like Hagar, God asked me to go back into a situation that I had found deeply painful – and had basically run away from. Even now, although I have experienced complete restoration, there are times when that pain tries to rise to the surface. Sometimes God asks us to step into places that are difficult. He never promised us a trouble-free life – in fact, Jesus Himself said: "In this world you will have trouble. But take heart! I have overcome the world" (John 16:33).

I believe that what truly makes a difference is being noticed and seen by God, which is what seemed to fuel Hagar's obedience. Once again, after being sent away and overcome with such anguish that she was no longer thinking straight, God showed Hagar that He had seen her and heard her son's cries (21:17). She was simply waiting for Ishmael to die, but God appeared and reiterated His promise, as well as providing practical help. Are there times in your own life where you feel like hope is lost, the wait is too long? Remember, God *does* see you – look around for His touch even in the waiting.

For prayer and reflection

Lord, thank You for the reminder that even in the seasons when I am struggling You do see me, and You look out for me. Help me to recognise Your hand at work. Amen.

In need of **maturing**

Genesis 37:3–28

'Joseph had a dream, and when he told it to his brothers, they hated him all the more.' (v5)

There are times in our lives when, in all honesty, God's 'not yet' is about maturing our character. He is far more interested in shaping us to be more like His Son than our comfort, which can be difficult to accept at times. But this story is a reminder of how God can sometimes reveal His plans to us and then we run away with them, or are foolish in whom we tell. Rather than keeping the dreams to himself, Joseph, who was already very aware he was his dad's favourite, couldn't help but tell his brothers. The result? Their jealousy caused them to sell him into slavery.

We may not experience something quite so disastrous as a result of our own immaturity, but we can probably recall a time when we didn't react wisely when God revealed plans to us that were for our future rather than right then. I remember how Mary, caught up in the whirlwind of giving birth to God's Son, and seeing shepherds and wise men come to worship the baby, treasured up all these things and pondered them in her heart' (Luke 2:19). I can be impatient, impulsive and desperate to act on what God reveals to me – in these times He reminds me of Mary's gentle, quiet response. I recognise that some of my frustrations with periods of waiting can be because I want to see the fruition of something that God has told me. And yet my mum modelled so well how to wait patiently, and to continue to bring His promises to Him in prayer. She prayed for over 30 years for my dad's salvation, based on a scriptural promise God had given her, and died passing on the mantle to myself and my sister.

For prayer and reflection

Lord, help me to be wise and keep in step with Your timing, rather than trying to run ahead. And help me to submit to Your moulding of my character. Amen.

Imprisoned

Genesis 39: 16–23

'But while Joseph was there in the prison, the LORD was with him' (vv20–21)

Joseph was faithful in his position as servant in Potiphar's household, which shows a deepening level of maturity. I can think of times when I have been placed in circumstances that I think are unfair – my response was not like Joseph's! How bewildering it must have been to be falsely accused and end up in prison! And yet we are told that, again, God was with him and granted him favour. I wonder how often we don't see the blessing of God because we are too busy complaining about our circumstances?

Thinking about prison imagery, I believe that sometimes we can make our own 'prisons' because we hold on to unforgiveness and bitterness. At other times we are in 'prisons' of ill health, difficult relationships, broken dreams. How do we handle those? My mum clung on to her faith in the midst of debilitating illnesses. When she first became housebound, she viewed it as being trapped at home with a non-Christian. But she learned to be grateful for the times she could sit with her Bible and pray for those God had placed on her heart. (Having initially felt useless, God revealed to her that she was one of His prayer warriors.) Her relationship with dad also blossomed and deepened.

I am challenged by how well she waited until, ultimately, her wait was over and she met Jesus. But there are others who spur me on, too. I think of a writer friend who, because of the pandemic, had to shield away from her family due to chronic illness. While it was a desperately difficult time, she didn't allow that 'prison' to limit her: it was a year of prolific writing, and various projects were birthed and published.

For prayer and reflection

Lord, I am challenged by the changing attitude in Joseph. Too often, I can complain rather than faithfully serve where I am, despite the difficulties.

Raised up at the right moment

THURS **FEB 10**

Genesis 41: 14–16, 41–57

'It is because God has made me fruitful in the land of my suffering.' (v52)

The cupbearer Joseph had met in prison finally spoke up, bringing Joseph to the attention of the one person who could immediately release him (vv9–13). Notice that Joseph's character had changed immensely by this point – rather than feeling puffed up that Pharaoh was expecting him to interpret his troubling dream, he simply said, 'I cannot do it... but God' (v16). What a change!

In response to the interpretation, Joseph was raised up as high as he could possibly be, and yet the lessons he had learned (presumably the hard way) while in prison remained. He served Pharaoh and the nation of Egypt faithfully and wisely, preparing the whole area for the coming famine. But he also recognised that it was God's doing, and noted the fruit produced within his suffering – choosing to acknowledge this in the name he chose for his second-born, Ephraim. How often do we try to rush past seasons of suffering, without asking God what fruit He is producing within us? A challenging but vital question to ask ourselves. I have learned to pause before asking for rescue in hard times, and ask God if there is anything He is wanting to teach me, or change in me, first.

Joseph's brothers were sent to Egypt to find food during the famine, and he ended up being reconciled with them and his father (see Gen. 45:1–20). His story reminds me of Esther's, found in the book of Esther. She came to recognise she had been raised up 'for such a time as this' (Esth. 4:14). May we too know God's perspective in each season of life, whether we are suffering, waiting for a particular answer to prayer or in a time of plenty and rest.

For prayer and reflection

Lord, I am challenged by the faithfulness of your servants, Joseph and Esther. May I recognise Your hand at work in my life, and the fruit you are producing too. Amen.

Exodus 2:11–25

'Moses fled from Pharaoh and went to live in Midian' (v15)

Moses' time of **waiting**

At the end of Genesis, God moved 70 members of what was originally Abraham's family (Jacob and his descendants) to Egypt (through what happened to Joseph) with the express purpose of making His nation great. Yet there is a gap of almost 400 years between Genesis and Exodus and, while Abraham's descendants had grown numerous, they were in captivity in Egypt. So what happened to God's master plan? What a long period of waiting. God still saw the Israelites, but had they lost hope in His promise of rescue under the weight of oppression?

Enter Moses; miraculously saved from the ruling pharaoh's evil decree by pharaoh's own daughter, he ended up spending his childhood in the palace (Exod. 2:10). When grown up, Moses was incensed by the mistreatment of Hebrews, and killed an Egyptian. Having to flee, he ended up living in Midian for 40 years, where God prepared him for his rescue mission (interestingly, reflecting the same period of time the Israelites wandered in the desert for).

Moses' first action in Midian was to rescue Reuel's daughters. This echoed what he would eventually do for the Israelites: stand up for them, and provide water in the wildness. He became a shepherd in Midian – it may not seem like the obvious training ground for leadership, but remember the great King David started off as a shepherd boy too. Nothing was wasted during Moses' time of personal exile, which is an important truth to take on board in our own lives. What started off as a result of a rather enormous mistake, became the vital springboard for his leadership development.

For prayer and reflection

Lord, I thank You for the reminder that You never waste any moment in our lives – including the consequences of our own mistakes. Amen.

Waiting well

Psalm 37:1–11

'Be still before the LORD and wait patiently for him.' (v7)

This psalm gives us some great insights into how to wait well. We are told to 'be still' and 'wait patiently' – the latter we will unpack later. But we are also told to wait without getting fretful, being angry or turning to wrath. Why? Because, as we are reminded in verse nine, God is ultimately in control. Looking forward to our eternity with Him can help us consider the frustrations of the present in the light of this perspective.

Rather than allowing ourselves to ruminate on our difficulties, we can choose to fix our eyes on Him. As it says in verse four, 'Take delight in the LORD' – learn more about Him, take time to dwell in His presence. Why not take some time to brainstorm what delighting in God could look like for you in your current circumstances?

While being still before God is vital as it renews us, this psalm also shows us that waiting is active: 'Trust in the LORD and do good; dwell in the land' (v3). 'Doing good' and 'dwelling' remind me that we are called to be those our neighbours are pleased to have living near them. How can you bless those around you today?

Optional further reading

Psalm 46:10

MON **FEB 14**

40 years of **wandering**

Exodus 15:22–27

'The people grumbled against Moses' (v24)

Moses was called by God through extraordinary means (a burning bush, see Exod. 3), and then, against what seemed like impossible odds, God displayed His power by taking on the Egyptian gods and providing an incredible escape for His people (Exod. 14). God then undertook the careful, painstaking process of taking Egypt out of *them*. The result of hundreds of years of captivity had caused unhelpful influences in their lives. God's deepest desire was to dwell with His people – it still is – and yet His glory and holiness demanded that they learn to live holy lives.

There is a progression, and sense of ongoing journey, in the book of Exodus. Yes, the obvious journey from Egypt to Mount Sinai, and the ongoing journey in the wilderness. But this is parallelled with the Israelites' journey towards God, as they learned how to be His chosen people. He provided them with revelation, though this was a process too (and still is for us). God has rescued us through Jesus – yet how often do we slip back into an 'Egypt' mentality, to old, unhelpful habits?

The Israelites had to learn a whole new way of living, trusting God for daily provision. It took them time, and they fell into grumbling very easily (anyone else do that?!). We need to heed the lessons of Exodus and remember to trust God for all we need – physically, emotionally and spiritually. Their journey could have taken just 11 days, but took 40 years! We, too, may journey through what seems like wilderness times, and yet we can trust in God's timing and submit to His will so that our waiting has purpose.

For prayer and reflection

Lord, I remember Your incredible provision, but am sobered by how long it took for Your people to reach the Promised Land. Help me to journey with You always. Amen.

Pouring out her **pain**

Hannah was in deep distress, and dealing with her rival's cruel jealousy. I know there will be those reading this who have experienced, and may still be experiencing, the intense heartbreak of childlessness. I pray that you may know God's comfort and care in such a difficult time.

Whatever particular grief or anguish you may be experiencing, may I gently suggest that you can take your pain and your tears and pour it all out before God. Here we see a woman unafraid to ugly cry in front of her God – and anyone else watching. There have been moments in recent years where the extraordinary depths of pain and grief have wracked my body and soul, and I have been unable to do anything but sob my heart out. But I have had to make the choice either to do that before my God, or try to hide from Him. In all honesty, there have been moments of both – although I know He always sees us. However, when I have come before Him I have certainly felt less alone.

The hardest thing can be when we are misunderstood in our grief – and in our waiting – as Hannah was here. How difficult it must have been, for the man of God to assume she was drunk! Sometimes, other well-meaning Christians can say and do similar things to us when they misread situations or our behaviour. That can cause us to question ourselves, and even God. Let's not allow our responses to be based on our treatment from others. Like Hannah, we know in our hearts whether we have become bitter or if we are staying soft towards God. Let's not be swayed away from keeping our eyes fixed on God, however painful it is right now.

1 Samuel 1:1–20

'Do not take your servant for a wicked woman; I have been praying here out of my great anguish and grief.' (v16)

For prayer and reflection

I am grateful for the example of those, like Hannah, who poured out their anguish readily before You. Help me to be open to You about all my thoughts and feelings. Amen.

Anointed yet **pursued**

1 Samuel 24:1–20

'The LORD forbid that I should do such a thing to my master, the LORD's anointed' (v6)

David was singled out by God for what was in his heart, and anointed to be the next king of Israel (1 Sam. 16), yet he didn't gain the throne immediately (2 Sam. 5). He ended up running from the reigning king, Saul, who was trying to take his life, although David had always served him faithfully.

David took to the hills, and hid in caves. And although he was living in basic, difficult circumstances, he drew followers to himself: in 1 Samuel 22:2, we read that 400 men had joined him. By 1 Samuel 23:13, that number had risen to around 600! Imagine that – God was working on David's leadership qualities in the secret, hidden places. If he had sent those people away, or waited until Saul agreed to hand over the crown, David would never have continued the leadership 'apprenticeship scheme' God had started as he laid down his life to protect those sheep in his teenage years. Do we wait for recognition from others, or for circumstances to seem appropriate before stepping into all God has for us? Do we perhaps hinder the preparation process God is trying to outwork in us, and thereby unintentionally prolong our own waiting? It is worth considering what our attitude is to the circumstances we find ourselves in.

I also find it challenging that even though David was being told by those around him that God had obviously delivered Saul into his hands, in his heart he knew that this wasn't the time – or even for him to do. He was tuned into God's heart enough to recognise that, and humble enough even to apologise to the man who was after his life! Whose voices are we listening to in the waiting?

For prayer and reflection

Take some time to think about what David's story (from being anointed to finally taking the throne) can teach you about your own life today. What challenges you the most?

Even if...

Daniel 3:8–28

'The God we serve is able to deliver us from it… But even if he does not… we will not serve your gods' (vv17–18)

I have been drawn back to the story of Shadrach, Meshach and Abednego many times in the last few years, particularly in times of intense pressure or pain when it can be so easy to question God and wonder why He is allowing what is going on to happen. I find two declarations increasingly come to mind: the Israelites' bold statement in today's key verses; and Peter's reply to Jesus, 'To whom shall we go? You have the words of eternal life' (John 6:68), when Jesus asked the disciples if they wanted to desert him, as so many others were doing.

These men were in a life or death situation. The king had made a decree and there was a real, physical furnace they would be thrown into if they disobeyed. We might not be faced with exactly that, but often we have a choice whether to blend into the norms of our culture, or to stick out while standing up for Christian values. People can question why we still believe in God when we have had to cope with so much suffering. That was one of the causes of arguments in my own home, with dad wondering why mum continued to cling to her faith. And it is the continuing stumbling block for him.

I love the miracle that occurs in this story: not only are the three men alive and unsinged, but there is a fourth person in the fire with them. Could that have been Jesus? It was certainly a supernatural being. Often I wish that God would do something so miraculous that those around me would have to acknowledge His existence. But I know, above all, I am called to live simply and humbly, whatever my circumstances, in a way that reveals Him to those I am in contact with.

For prayer and reflection

Lord, I am challenged by the resolute faith of these men, in the face of what looked like certain death. Help me not to be swayed by the pressures I face today. Amen.

FRI **FEB 18**

A **spiritual** fight

Daniel 10:1–14

'The prince of the Persian kingdom resisted me twenty-one days.' (v13)

Daniel remained steadfast and faithful although he was living in exile. God also revealed things to him supernaturally, including the interpretation of dreams. Here we find that he had been crying out to God, praying for His people, but also humbling himself and acknowledging his own sin. And yet there was a delay in the answer to his prayers – why?

We have concentrated on how God uses times of waiting to mould our characters, and yet there is another reason that God's answers can be delayed – the spiritual battle raging around us. We know that 'our struggle is not against flesh and blood, but against the rulers, against the authorities, against the powers of this dark world and against the spiritual forces of evil in the heavenly realms' (Eph. 6:12). In this passage, Daniel is clearly told that as soon as he started praying God heard his prayers and sent the messenger that Daniel was seeing in his vision (see v12). However, he was held up for 21 days by a battle taking place in the spiritual realm.

We can shy away from talking about the forces of darkness, and it is prudent to be cautious. However, not every delay is God simply saying wait. We do have an enemy who hates us to make progress. Have you noticed when you step out in faith and/or achieve great things in God's name, it can often feel that life suddenly throws all sorts of curveballs at you? Our enemy doesn't like being pushed back, and he can certainly try to resist what God is doing. It is helpful to bear this in mind, and also to put on the full armour of God that is described in Ephesians 6 in order to stand strong.

For prayer and reflection

Take some time to read Ephesians 6:10–18, visualising actually putting on each piece of armour. Thank God for the gift of each piece, and commit to standing strong today.

Sheltered in God

Psalm 27

'For in the day of trouble… he will hide me in the shelter of his sacred tent' (v5)

This psalm is packed full of rich truth. We are told to 'be strong and take heart' (v14) as we wait for God's rescue, but David reminds himself at the start not to allow fear to overwhelm him. With so much going on (an army approaching) it could be so easy to look at circumstances and be gripped by fear. I know I've done that. And yet he reminds himself, and us, in that time of waiting to ask for God's presence first (v4) – how often do we forget that, in our haste to ask for rescue? We read how God shelters us and keeps us safe even in 'the day of trouble' (v5) – God may not take away the danger or the difficulty, but offers shelter within it.

As a family, we have gone through some intensely difficult times, in which I have cried out for God's mercy and deliverance. As a worship leader, I have had to determine, as David did: 'I will sacrifice with shouts of joy; I will sing and make music to the LORD' (v6). It has certainly been a sacrifice and yet, as I have worshipped, God has brought peace to my troubled soul. Although the wait continues, He offers strength and renewal.

Optional further reading

Psalm 25

MON **FEB 21**

A **focused** heart

Luke 2:36–38

'She never left the temple but worshipped night and day, fasting and praying.' (v37)

Where do we 'live' when we are waiting? Do we keep all our focus on that one thing we are crying out for, or do we live in a way that reveals we value the presence of God above everything else? Anna experienced such sorrow and heartache through becoming a widow after just seven short years. And yet we are told she never left the temple, but instead worshipped, prayed and fasted. Like Simeon, she is described as a prophet, and I am sure she would have been aware of the fact that he had been promised that he wouldn't die before seeing the Messiah (see Luke 2:26). I imagine she was expectant of seeing the Messiah, too, as a result. And she is now in our Bibles as one of the first people to spread the news about Jesus. What an honour!

At times, I can give up on spiritual disciplines when things are hard. Yet I also know the power of prayer and worship to lift my spirit as well as my gaze. I have been drawn to fasting too, as I pray for breakthrough in particular situations. Jesus Himself said, 'When you fast' (Matt. 6:16) – so expects us to. Although His own disciples did not fast, as He was with them, He did indicate they would do so once He left (Matt. 9:14–17). If fasting is not a part of your life right now, can I encourage you to try it? I usually fast just one meal – and you can fast from things other than food too (particularly if you have a medical reason for not abstaining from food).

It's worth noting Anna's response once she had seen the child – she thanked God. I wonder how often we forget to do that when we do eventually receive the answers we have been longing for?

For prayer and reflection

Lord, there is so much in these few verses that is challenging. I want to be one who worships you day and night – help me to cultivate that attitude in my heart. Amen.

Even **Jesus**...

TUES **FEB 22**

Luke 4:1–13

'Jesus… was led by the Spirit into the wilderness, where for forty days he was tempted by the devil.' (vv1–2)

I recently saw a social media post about the seed of the Chinese bamboo tree. It takes five years for the seed to sprout from the ground and every single day it must be watered and fed fertiliser or it dies. From the outside it looks like nothing is happening, but the tree is developing an extensive root system, putting solid foundations in place. In the fifth year it grows 80–90 feet in just five or six weeks! In our seasons of waiting. are we taking care of ourselves and putting down strong roots?

When we look back over Jesus' life, He spent 30 years waiting before His short, intense three-year ministry. As a child we know He grew up obeying His parents and that He 'grew in wisdom and stature' (Luke 2:52). If Jesus needed to grow and develop, how much more so do we?!

But what can we learn about His time in the wilderness, when He was hungry and tired? He had just been baptised, and God had affirmed His identity (Luke 3:22). Then note that it was the Spirit who led Him to the wilderness. Once there, He was tempted by the devil. We need to recognise that this can happen to us when we are feeling depleted. But Jesus was sure of who He was, and sure of the Word of God, so was able to refute every lie and temptation that was put to Him. This challenges me to remember how important knowing and rooting my identity in God is, but also having scriptures to hand that I can use to bat away unhelpful thoughts, feelings and temptations before they take root. And we have His words to simply cling to in those most heartbreaking of times of waiting and crying out for breakthrough.

For prayer and reflection

Lord, I recognise that sometimes I am too eager to move past the times of preparation, but that they help me grow and develop. Help me to root myself firmly in You. Amen.

WED **FEB 23**

Reaching out in **desperation**

Luke 8:43–48

'She came up behind him and touched the edge of his cloak' (v44)

We are not told this woman's name, but what we do know is that for 12 long years she had battled a hugely debilitating, but also shaming, illness. Menstruating women were seen as unclean and so she would have been looked upon as such for all those years. And yet, when Jesus finally came to within touching distance, she still had a choice. Break the ceremonial laws by reaching out to touch him, or simply let Him pass by. It would have taken a mixture of courage and desperation to do what she did – ever felt like that? I know I have 'touched' Him with my own desperate prayers, and I think that, like she did, it shows that we are still exercising faith. Indeed, He spoke kindly to her, saying: 'Daughter, your faith has healed you. Go in peace' (v48).

There is much about healing and miracles that I don't understand, and have wrestled with over the years, having seen some at work in my mum's life but, ultimately, watching her slowly deteriorate and die. And I think we can heap judgment on people who don't get healed, when we talk about levels of faith. Yet Jesus here so clearly says that the woman's faith healed her. There is a link between healing and faith – and I think a lot of it has to do with our words and actions reflecting a belief that, as Shadrach, Meshach and Abednego asserted, our God can heal. Sometimes our faith is about continuing to stand firm when that healing is delayed, or doesn't come. If that is your experience right now, I would like to pray this over you: 'May the God of hope fill you with all joy and peace as you trust in him' (Rom. 15:13).

For prayer and reflection

Visualise yourself as the woman in the crowd who reaches out to touch Jesus' cloak. What is it that you are hoping He will do for you today? Take that request before Him.

Next Issue

MAR/APR 2022

March

REVELATION

AMY BOUCHER PYE

April

REFLECTIVE ROUTINE AND RADICAL REST

NAOMI AIDOO

Available in a variety of formats

In **March**, join Amy Boucher Pye for a journey through the vision of John, the ageing disciple, which is sometimes puzzling but ultimately faith building.

In **April**, Naomi Aidoo takes us on a journey in both purpose and pause, exploring the importance which one has on the other as we look at how both intentional routine and deliberate rest shape much of who we are as Christ followers.

Obtain your copy from waverleyabbeyresources.org

Learning to be **persistent**

Luke 18:1–8

'Will not God bring about justice for his chosen ones, who cry out to him day and night?' (v7)

The parable of the persistent widow is one Jesus told to reveal to the disciples (and us) that 'they should always pray and not give up' (v1). When we have waited for days, months or even years, we do get weary and it can be all too easy to stop being as faithful or fervent with our prayers as we were when we first started.

In January 2021 I was feeling weary: it was coming up to the one-year anniversary of my mum's death, we had been leading our church through the pandemic for many months – and our daughter was beginning to show signs of mental ill-health. My dad had again categorically stated that he would never believe. Right at that time, God brought a family going through an unbelievably difficult journey into our lives. Out of the blue, Hannah Montague experienced a severe brain bleed, which left her in a coma. She was 23 and had only been married four and half months to husband Rob An online family from around the world was raised up to pray morning and evening for her full healing. At the time of writing, it is almost nine months later, and we have seen her progress from being given two days to live to being in a rehab facility where she is responding well, but yet to be fully restored.

Her father, Royston Young, told me this parable has been brought to life in a new way, and commented: 'It has been truly amazing to see that in all the pain of waiting, there has been a waking of the family's faith and those coming together to pray. It's almost as if we are the ones really waking up from our slumber.' The faith of this family and others has really challenged and lifted me.

For prayer and reflection

While it can be hard to bring the same prayer requests before God day after day, thank Him for the reminder to be persistent before lifting your requests once more.

Affirming our faith in Jesus

John 11:1–6, 17–27

'When he heard that Lazarus was ill, he stayed where he was two more days' (v6)

This is the passage that I have been drawn to again and again recently, particularly in times of grief. Mary, Martha and Lazarus were siblings, and riends of Jesus. The sisters obviously felt the depth of elationship, as they asked Jesus to rush back to heal heir brother. But we see that Jesus' response was to vait another few days before travelling back to Bethany.

Jesus knew that this was the time God had ordained or Him to show He had power over death itself – but the isters didn't! How perplexing and excruciatingly painful : must have been, as they went through the agony of heir brother dying and Jesus not being there in time.

When Martha went to meet Jesus, she immediately onfronted Him (see v21). How often have you prayed imilar prayers: 'Lord, if You had just moved when I sked, this would not have happened...'? Yet Martha ollows it with a statement of faith, in verse 22. It was at is point that Jesus encouraged her to exercise her faith ven more, by revealing that He is 'the resurrection and e life' (v25), interestingly *before* He raised Lazarus.

Katherine Gantlett has written about her seasons f loss and waiting, including giving birth to a stillborn nd having five miscarriages, in *Walking through Winter* nstant Apostle). She told me that, 'Our losses revealed l the cracks in how I thought about God, how his power orks, who I am and who or what I was looking to for alvation and healing.'

Perhaps God is asking us to look at where we are acing our trust, and reminding us to vocalise our ith in His redeeming love and power, whatever our rcumstances.

For prayer and reflection

John 11 contains the shortest verse in the Bible: 'Jesus wept' (v35). Do remember, even when He is waiting to move, He still cares and weeps alongside you in your pain.

Weekend

Soaring with God

Isaiah 40:28–31

'those who hope in the LORD will renew their strength.' (v31).

All of us get weary at times, and so it is good to remember that our God never does, and that He can provide strength and power to us (v29). We do get physically, emotionally and spiritually depleted – do we recognise it when we do and take time to wait on Him?

I was looking at these verses when I noticed author Kate Nicholas commenting on them on social media. She was undergoing chemotherapy for her second bout of cancer and found her attention was being drawn to focus on the idea of waiting on God, particularly the Hebrew word *Qavah*, used in these verses, which means to actively wait with anticipation. She told me: 'Cancer has a lot to teach us about waiting upon God. It strips us of our sense of control and forces us into a time of waiting; for treatment, tests, for results, for God's will to be done. We spend our whole lives in action, trying to control the space and time we inhabit. But when we wait we stand on holy ground; a place of surrender to God; a place of recognition of our lack of control. It is humbling, but is pregnant with opportunity.' I love that last phrase.

Optional further reading

2 Corinthians 4:7–18; Hebrews 12:1–3

Waiting patiently with **hope**

MON **FEB 28**

James 5:7–11, Romans 5:1–5

'Be patient, then, brothers and sisters, until the Lord's coming.' (James 5:7)

As we end this month's reflections, let's look at James' description of what waiting well looks like. He talks about waiting patiently four imes here and yet, as we've noted previously, we can often look for instant fixes and miss out on what God s teaching us. While writing this, I was drawn back to Romans 5, where we are told 'that suffering produces perseverance; perseverance, character; and character, hope' (vv3–4). We don't like to dwell on it, but the truth s that hope often comes from a process that includes both suffering and patience.

The farmer in James' passage recognised that easons change – as will things in our lives. Author athy Madavan commented in a talk she gave: 'There often a season of barrenness before a season of hope nd so many of us get fixated about the future that we orget about waiting well now. The reality is that it is the hoices we make now that will be so much part of the efinition of our future. This moment is a gift as we can now God as we wait well."

Just as Kate Nicholas explained, we *always* have opportunities to meet with God, and to grow more like is Son. Let us remember that one day God will '"wipe very tear from their eyes. There will be no more death" mourning or crying or pain' (Rev. 21:4). While it may e difficult, we *can* wait with patience because we have e hope of what is to come. That is something to rejoice , even while we need God's help to stop negative elings and frustrations taking our attention. Remember, timately 'the battle is not yours, but God's' (2 Chron.):15).

For prayer and reflection

Thank God for all He has revealed to you in this study and, today, choose to actively 'look to the LORD our God, till he shows [you] his mercy' (Psa. 123:2).

Order form

IWED J/F 2022

Get Your FREE Daily Bible Reading Notes TODAY! (UK ONLY)

Your favourite Bible reading notes are now FREE. God has called us back to the original vision of CWR to provide these notes to everyone who needs them, regardless of their circumstance or ability to pay. It is our desire to see these daily Bible reading notes used more widely, to see Christians grow in their relationship with Jesus on a daily basis and to see Him reflected in their everyday living. Clearly there are costs to provide this ministry and we are trusting in God's provision.

Could you be part of this vision? Do you have the desire to see lives transformed through a relationship with Jesus? **A small donation from you of just £2 a month, by direct debit, will make such a difference** Giving hope to someone in desperate need whilst you too grow deeper in your own relationship with Jesus.

4 Easy Ways To Order

1. Visit our online store at **waverleyabbeyresources.org/store**
2. Send this form together with your payment to: **Waverley Abbey Trust, Waverley Abbey House, Waverley Lane, Farnham, Surrey GU9 8EP**
3. Phone in your credit card order: **01252 784700** (Mon–Fri, 9.30am – 4.30pm)
4. Visit a Christian bookshop

or a list of our National Distributors, who supply countries outside the UK, visit waverleyabbeyresources.org/distributors

Your Details (required for orders and donations)

Full Name: **ID No.** (if known):

Home Address:

Postcode:

Telephone No. (for queries): **Email:**

Publications

TITLE	QTY	PRICE	TOTAL
TOTAL PUBLICATIONS			

UK P&P: up to £24.99 = **£2.99**; £25.00 and over = **FREE**

Elsewhere P&P: up to £10 = **£4.95**; £10.01 – £50 = **£6.95**; £50.01 – £99.99 = **£10**; £100 and over = **£30**

Total Publications and P&P (please allow 14 days for delivery) **A**

Payment Details

☐ I enclose a cheque made payable to CWR for the amount of: **£**

☐ Please charge my credit/debit card.

Cardholder's Name (in BLOCK CAPITALS)

Card No.

Expires End

Security Code

Continued overleaf >>

<< See previous page for start of order form

One off Special Gift to Waverley Abbey Trust

☐ Please send me an acknowledgement of my gift **B**

GRAND TOTAL (Total of A & B)

Gift Aid (your home address required, see overleaf)

giftaid it

I am a UK taxpayer and want CWR to reclaim the tax on all my donations for the four years prior to this yea **and on** all donations I make from the date of this Gift Aid declaration until further notice.*

Taxpayer's Full Name (in BLOCK CAPITALS) ____________

Signature ____________ **Date** ____________

*I am a UK taxpayer and understand that if I pay less Income Tax and/or Capital Gains Tax than the amount of Gift Aid claimed on all my donations in that ta year it is my responsibility to pay any difference.

Your FREE Daily Bible Reading Notes Order

Please Tick	FREE	£2 pcm	£5 pcm	£10 pcm	Other
Every Day with Jesus	☐	☐	☐	☐	☐ £ ____
Large Print *Every Day with Jesus*	☐	☐	☐	☐	☐ £ ____
Inspiring Women Every Day	☐	☐	☐	☐	☐ £ ____

All CWR Bible reading notes are also available in single issue **ebook** and **email subscription** format. Visit **waverleyabbeyresources.org** for further info

CWR **Instruction to your Bank or Building Society to pay by Direct Debit**

DIREC Debi

Please fill in the form and send to: CWR, Waverley Abbey House, Waverley Lane, Farnham, Surrey GU9 8EP

Name and full postal address of your Bank or Building Society

To: The Manager ____________ Bank/Building Society

Address ____________

Postcode

Originator's Identification Number

4	2	0	4	8	7

Reference

Instruction to your Bank or Building Society

Please pay CWR Direct Debits from the account detailed in this Instr subject to the safeguards assured by the Direct Debit Guarantee. I understand that this Instruction may remain with CWR and, if so, de will be passed electronically to my Bank/Building Society.

Signature(s)

Date

Name(s) of Account Holder(s)

Branch Sort Code

Bank/Building Society Account Number

Banks and Building Societies may not accept Direct Debit Instructions for some types of account

For a subscription outside of the UK please visit www.waverleyabbeyresources.o where you will find a list of our national distributors.

How would you like to hear from us? We would love to keep you up to date on all aspects of the CWR ministry, including; new publications, events & courses as well as how you can support us.

If you **DO** want to hear from us on email, please tick here [ ] If you **DO NOT** want us to contact you by post, please tick h

You can update your preferences at any time by contacting our customer services team on 01252 784 700. You can view our privacy policy online at waverleyabbeyresources.org